FAST Lane DRAG RACING

TOP FUEL DRAGSTERS

By Tyrone Georgiou

Gareth Stevens
Publishing

Please visit our Web site, www.garethstevens.com. For a free color catalog of all our high-quality books, call toll free 1-800-542-2595 or fax 1-877-542-2596.

Library of Congress Cataloging-in-Publication Data

Georgiou, Tyrone.
Top fuel dragsters / Tyrone Georgiou.
        p. cm. — (Fast lane. Drag racing)
Includes index.
ISBN 978-1-4339-4708-7 (pbk.)
ISBN 978-1-4339-4709-4 (6-pack)
ISBN 978-1-4339-4707-0 (library binding)
1. Drag racing—Juvenile literature. I. Title.
GV1029.3.G495 2011
796.72—dc22
                                            2010039130

First Edition

Published in 2011 by
Gareth Stevens Publishing
111 East 14th Street, Suite 349
New York, NY 10003

Designer: Daniel Hosek
Editor: Greg Roza

Photo credits: Cover, pp. 1, 17 Rusty Jarrett/Getty Images; p. 5 Alvin Upitis/Getty Images; pp. 7, 11 (main image), 12–13, 15, 19 (main image) Brian Bahr/Getty Images; p. 9 (main image) Getty Images; p. 9 (Garlits) Ken Levine/Getty Images; pp. 11 (Hill), 13 (inset) Jamie Squire/Getty Images; p. 19 (HANS device) Todd Warshaw/Getty Images.

Printed in the United States of America

CPSIA compliance information: Batch #CW11GS: For further information contact Gareth Stevens, New York, New York at 1-800-542-2595.

CONTENTS

Words in the glossary appear in **bold** type the first time they are used in the text.

One type of drag racing car was based on the Ford and Chevrolet cars of the 1930s and 1940s. Drivers made the cars lighter by removing parts they didn't need for racing. Pretty soon, they were down to just the frame, engine, wheels, steering wheel, and driver's seat! They moved the driver's seat back over the rear wheels and lengthened the frame to provide better steering and control. These first dragsters became known as "rail jobs." Over time, they changed into today's Top Fuel dragsters.

Top Fuel racing has long been a favorite with racing fans.

SUPERCHARGED!

The **V-8 engine** of a Top Fuel dragster is supercharged—it's made to create extra power. It produces 8,000 **horsepower** (HP)! All that power is channeled to wide, smooth racing tires called "slicks." Top fuel dragsters race down a ¼-mile (400-m) track in less than 4 seconds, reaching a speed of 320 miles (515 km) per hour! A normal car produces about 150 HP and travels ¼ mile in 12 to 15 seconds. Top Fuel dragsters have so much power they make the ground shake during a race.

Fast Fact A Top Fuel dragster engine can only produce 8,000 horsepower for a few seconds before the engine actually destroys itself and explodes. Good thing a race only takes 4 seconds!

Regular car brakes aren't enough to slow down a Top Fuel dragster. Just like a skydiver, it needs parachutes to slow it down!

SWAMP RATS

Don "Big Daddy" Garlits is known as the father of the Top Fuel dragster. Over the years, he created some of the most important **innovations** for the sport. His series of cars, called Swamp Rats, shows how Top Fuel cars changed into those used today.

In 1958, Swamp Rat 1 set a world speed record of 180 miles (290 km) per hour. In 1986, Swamp Rat 30 set a new speed record of 272.56 miles (438.64 km) per hour!

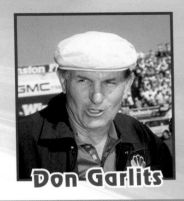

Don Garlits

Swamp Rat 30, shown here in 1986, is now on display at the Smithsonian Institution in Washington, D.C.

TOP FUEL DRAGSTER PARTS

A Top Fuel dragster is 25 feet (7.6 m) long. A 20-gallon (75-L) fuel tank holds just enough fuel for one race. The body is made of lightweight plates. A metal frame called a roll cage surrounds the driver in case the car flips over!

The tiny front wheels are used for steering. The 17-inch (43-cm) rear wheels provide all the power. Top Fuel dragsters also have front and rear parts called wings that help keep the car on the track.

Fast Fact

Eddie Hill—known to fans as "Fast Eddie"—was the first Top Fuel racer to have an **elapsed time** (ET) in the 4-second range. He became a National Hot Rod Association (NHRA) National Champion in 1993 at age 57—the oldest one ever.

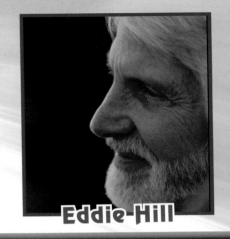

Eddie Hill

The wings on a Top Fuel dragster are similar to airplane wings. However, instead of lifting the car up, the wings use the force of rushing air to keep the car down on the track.

wings

wings

Before a race, water is placed on part of the track. The drivers **rev** their engines up to almost full power and drive through it. This is called a "burnout." It's done to heat up the tires and the track so the cars get good **traction** at the start of the race.

The drivers get into position at the starting line with the help of lights on the **starting tree**. Drivers can't cross the starting line until the lights on the tree turn green.

Fans love burnouts because they create a lot of smoke and noise.

starting tree

13

GREEN LIGHT!

When the lights turn green, you want to leave the starting line first. However, you also need to keep the car under control. Giving the rear wheels too much power too quickly can cause them to spin in place. Then you'll be going nowhere while the other racer speeds away. Spinning tires can hurt your engine, too. You also need to steer the car down the track in a straight line and not lose control. All this happens in less than 4 seconds!

Racers Antron Brown (left) and Tony Schumacher speed down the track at Infineon Raceway in Sonoma, California.

Fast Fact When speeding down the racetrack, Top Fuel racers experience a lot of force. It pushes them down in their seat at 6 times their regular weight. Pilots flying fighter jet planes sometimes black out when experiencing a force 7 times their regular weight!

15

BETWEEN RACES

A single race completely destroys the dragster's engine, so it goes back to the garage to be rebuilt for the next race. This takes about 75 minutes. A team of **mechanics** strips down the car. They take the engine apart and put in new parts. They repack the parachutes and refuel the car with a special fuel called **nitromethane**. Any mistake could lead to major problems. Then it's back to the track to race again.

Fast Fact "TV Tommy" Ivo was a drag racer and television actor who set many national records. He built some wild machines trying to get a horsepower advantage on the track, including a 4-engine dragster in 1961. Unfortunately, the NHRA banned it from racing.

Tony Schumacher's team gives his dragster one last check before a race.

17

TOP FUEL DRAGSTER SAFETY

Top Fuel dragsters are powerful machines. Although drivers are very skillful, accidents do happen. Fire from exploding engines and loss of control from breaking parts are huge dangers. Nitromethane fuel is very explosive, so drivers wear special racing suits that don't burn. Each car has a driver-controlled system to stop fires. The five-point safety harness, or seat belt, and the roll cage help stop the driver from being thrown from the car during a crash.

Fast Fact The HANS (head and neck support) device is worn by drivers in all types of racing. It helps prevent the head and neck injuries that result from sudden changes in speed, such as those a crash causes.

HANS-device

Cory McClenathan's engine explodes just as he crosses the finish line!

19

CHAMPS!

Shirley Muldowney is the "First Lady" of drag racing. She was the first woman to drive a Top Fuel dragster and the first to become an NHRA National Champion in 1977.

Kenny Bernstein, the "King of Speed," was the first man to hit 300 miles (483 km) per hour on a ¼-mile track. He holds two NHRA Top Fuel Championships and 39 career wins.

During a **qualifying race** in 2005, Tony Schumacher set the fastest speed ever recorded in NHRA history: 337.58 miles (543.28 km) per hour!

TOP FUEL NUMBERS

Fastest ET	**3.771 seconds, Tony Schumacher, 10/12/08**
Fastest Officially Recognized Speed	**324.98 mph (523 kmh), Tony Schumacher, 3/14/10**
Most Wins	**64, Tony Schumacher**
First Top Fuel Champion	**Gary Beck**
Most Championships	**7, Tony Schumacher** (including six in a row from 2004 to 2009)

GLOSSARY

elapsed time (ET): the amount of time it takes to get from the starting line to the finish line

horsepower (HP): the measure of the power produced by an engine

innovation: a new invention, or a new way of doing things

mechanic: a person who works on cars

nitromethane: a powerful fuel used in rockets and dragsters

qualifying race: one of a series of races held to see which drivers will advance to the final races

rev: to increase the speed of the engine

starting tree: a pole that holds the starting lights, which stick out like branches on a tree. Also called the Christmas tree.

traction: the stickiness between two surfaces, such as a tire and the track

V-8 engine: a motor where the two banks of cylinders are arranged in a V shape

FOR MORE INFORMATION

Books

Miller, Timothy. *Drag Racing: The World's Fastest Sport*. Buffalo, NY: Firefly Books, 2009.

Von Finn, Denny. *Top Fuel Dragsters*. Minneapolis, MN: Bellwether Media, 2010.

Web Sites

International Hot Rod Association (IHRA)

www.ihra.com
Read about drag racing at the Web site for the second-largest drag racing governing body.

The National Hot Rod Association (NHRA)

www.nhra.com
The Web site for the largest drag racing governing body has information on the hottest Top Fuel drivers.

Don Garlits

garlits.com
Read all about Don "Big Daddy" Garlits and see his historic Swamp Rats.

INDEX